SPIRITUAL GARMENTS

Prophet Sampson Amoateng

Prophet Sampson Amoateng

CONTENTS

INTRODUCTION

One of the common things we all do in life is to wear and change our clothing or garments. Changing your garment is part of your daily routine. From the day you are born until the day you die you will wear different clothes. There are garments you wear at home and others for different occasions. You have garments for school and garments for work. There are garments for weddings and garments for funerals. There are garments for sports games. Different sport teams also have different garments with diverse colors.

Again, based on the weather conditions you also change your dress. When it is winter we wear more and/or heavy clothing to keep ourselves warm and during summer we try to wear fewer and lighter clothes to avoid the heat.

In life, ordinarily, garments have different significance. Garments are identification systems. They are markers of identity. A police officer is known for his dressing. At times when you see people dressed in a certain way, you can tell whether they are male or female.

Garments are also used to signify our roles in life. When you go to a wedding party, no one must tell you who the bride is. Just based on her garment, you can identify her with ease.

Garments can tell us about your present experience and condition. When you wear funeral garments, it will signify that you are mourning. When you wear a graduation gown, it signifies you are done with school.

Garments and clothing also have vital significance in the realm of the spirit as revealed to us in the scriptures. In this masterpiece on spiritual garments, we will explore them and see the spiritual and deep mysteries of the scriptures. Read this book with a prophetic eye, and you will never remain the same again.

Prophet Sampson Amoateng

CHAPTER 1

SIGNIFICANCE OF GARMENTS

I believe if you were asked to guess the occupation of those in the above pictures you can do it with some level of certainty. Without being informed, you can guess accurately just based on the garments they are wearing.

The garments you wear physically reveals a lot about you. By the garments a person is wearing you can know and say a lot about them. Garments communicate to us. Garments can reveal one's occupation; they can reveal the present circumstance of a person. They can reveal the mood of a person or an event.

Again, the garments you wear dictates what happens to you. The garments you wear determines what you get and what you don't get. The garments you wear send a message to the world around you. The garments you wear can influence how people will treat you. The garments you wear physically can instill fear in people. Your garments cause people to form an opinion about you.

For example, when you meet a man dressed in dirty or tatty clothing with a bad odor, you may easily write him off as a beggar or even a mad person. You might be right or wrong, but his garments gave you an opinion.

SIGNIFICANCE OF SPIRITUAL GARMENTS

As is the natural so is the spiritual. There are parallels between the natural realm and the spiritual realm. In the realm of the spirit, one of the most important things you must work on is your garments. Garments speak a lot in the spiritual realm. In the realm of the spirit garments talk. I want to open your eyes to a certain dimension so that you know how this life operates.

THE FIRST THING THE ENEMY STEALS FROM YOU WHEN HE ATTACKS IS YOUR SPIRITUAL GARMENT

The Bible says the thief cometh not but to steal, to kill, and to destroy.

"The thief cometh not, but for to steal, and to kill, and to destroy: I am come that they might have life, and that they might have [it] more abundantly" (John 10:10 KJV)

The first thing the thief will do when he visits anyone is to take your garment.

"In reply Jesus said: "A man was going down from Jerusalem to Jericho, when he fell into the hands of robbers. They stripped him of his clothes, beat him and went away, leaving him half dead"
(Luke 10:30 KJV)

The devil is the greatest thief. In the parable of the good Samaritan, the first thing the robbers did when they met the traveler was to take away his garments. They stripped him of his precious garments.

Again, when the brothers of Joseph wanted to cast him into a pit and kill him, the first thing they did was to strip him of his garments-the coat of many colors.

"And it came to pass, when Joseph was come unto his brethren, that they stript Joseph out of his coat, [his] coat of

[many] colours that [was] on him; And they took him, and cast him into a pit: and the pit [was] empty, [there was] no water in it"(Genesis 37:23-24 KJV).

When Jesus was arrested by the soldiers to crucify him, the first thing they also did was to strip him of his garment or robe.

"Then the soldiers of the governor took Jesus into the common hall, and gathered unto him the whole band [of soldiers]. And they stripped him, and put on him a scarlet robe" (Matthew 27:27-28 KJV)

We must understand that in the realm of the spirit, till the enemy strips you of his garments he cannot hit you. Refuse to let the enemy strip you of your garments.

FOR YOUR LEVEL TO CHANGE IN LIFE YOUR SPIRITUAL GARMENTS MUST CHANGE

Your spiritual garments must change before

you experience a physical change. Blind Bartimaeus remained blind and a beggar all his life. But the day his status and position in society was about to change, the first thing which changed was his garments.

"And Jesus stood still, and commanded him to be called. And they call the blind man, saying unto him, Be of good comfort, rise; he calleth thee. And he, casting away his garment, rose, and came to Jesus. And Jesus answered and said unto him, What wilt thou that I should do unto thee? The blind man said unto him, Lord, that I might receive my sight. And Jesus said unto him, Go thy way; thy faith hath made thee whole. And immediately he received his sight, and followed Jesus in the way" (Mark 10:49-52 KJV)

Elisha who was a protégé of the prophet Elijah experienced a change of level the moment he received a new garment. That garment was the mantle of Elijah. Miraculous powers started operating in him greatly.

"He took up also the mantle of Elijah that fell from him, and went back, and stood by the bank of Jordan; And he took the mantle of Elijah that fell from him, and smote the waters, and said, Where [is] the LORD God of Elijah? and when he also had smitten the waters, they parted hither and thither: and Elisha went over" (2 Kings 2:13-14 KJV)

In one of the parables of Jesus, one man entered a wedding ceremony without wedding garments and he was cast out from there.

"And when the king came in to see the guests, he saw there a man which had not on a wedding garment: And he saith unto him, Friend, how camest thou in hither not having a wedding garment? And he was speechless. Then said the king to the servants, Bind him hand and foot, and take him away, and cast [him] into outer darkness; there shall be weeping and gnashing of teeth" (Matthew 22:11-13 KJV)

Friend, without the appropriate dress for the right level, you can't survive there. Many people get promoted and then later get demoted because spiritually they don't have the right spiritual garment consistent with that level.

GARMENTS TELL WHERE YOU ARE LOCATED SPIRITUALLY

The garments you wear in the realm of the spirit determine your level and ranking in this life. Your spiritual position is identified by your garments. Angels get to know your spiritual ranking by your garments. And the devils also, get to know your spiritual ranking by your garments. Just by seeing the quality of your garment your location is known.

Jesus declared that those who are dressed gorgeously live in the King's palaces.

"But what went ye out for to see? A man clothed in soft raiment? Behold, they which are gorgeously apparelled, and live

delicately, are in kings' courts" (Luke 7:25 KJV)

The New International Version of the Bible puts it this way:

"If not, what did you go out to see? A man dressed in fine clothes? No, those who wear expensive clothes and indulge in luxury are in palaces" (Luke 7:25 NIV)

Garments are a coding system in the spirit. When you wear garments which call for favor, favor will come to you. When you wear garments of death, death comes to you. Your spiritual garments tell us what must happen to you and what should not happen.

CHAPTER 2

JOSEPH AND HIS GARMENTS

I want to show you how garments determined the circumstances and the happenings in the life of Joseph. The garments of Joseph determined what happened to him and where he was allowed to stay. When you examine the garments of Joseph, you can conclude that 'garments make a man.' When he was given a garment, something happened to him and when a garment was taken from him, something happened to him. Joseph was demoted or promoted based on his garments.

Jacob had twelve sons who are known as the patriarchs. Joseph was the eleventh son. Among all of Jacob's children, Joseph was his father's favorite. He was loved especially by his dad.

"Now Israel loved Joseph more than all his children, because he [was] the son of his old age: and he made him a coat of [many] colors" (Genesis 37:3 KJV)

Joseph received a unique coat which showed how he was favored above all his brethren. The garment Joseph received made him stand out. The garment was a sign of extraordinary honor and privilege accorded to him by his father. Because of his unique garments, when all the other sons went to the field to look after the sheep, Joseph was exempted.

Now the same garments which were a sign of favor from his father became a token of hatred for him. It became very obvious to his brothers that he was loved by his father when they saw the garment of many colors. And the garments induced against Joseph hatred from his brothers.

"And when his brethren saw that their father loved him more than all his brethren, they hated him, and could not

speak peaceably unto him" (Genesis 37:4 KJV)

In the process of time, Joseph was sent by his father to check on his brothers in the field as they took care of sheep. When his brothers saw him coming, they sought to kill him because they were jealous of him and they hated him with great passion. When Joseph got to his brothers, the first thing they touched was his garment. They stripped him of his coat and put him inside a pit.

"And it came to pass, when Joseph was come unto his brethren, that they stript Joseph out of his coat, [his] coat of [many] colors that [was] on him" (Genesis 37:23 KJV)

As long as he wore his coat of many colors, he enjoyed favor, but the moment he lost it, he descended into a pit. Garments determine the happenings of man's life. As long as he wore that coat, he was a happy man. The day that coat left him his troubles began. He was cast naked into a pit and later sold into slavery.

"Then there passed by Midianites merchantmen; and they drew and lifted up Joseph out of the pit, and sold Joseph to the Ishmaelites for twenty [pieces] of silver: and they brought Joseph into Egypt" (Genesis 37:28 KJV)

As a slave, Joseph received slave garments. The man who was favored has become a slave because of changed garments.

As a slave, Joseph was carried into the house of Potiphar, an officer of Pharaoh in Egypt. Over there Potiphar's wife made sexual advances on Joseph. And because of the fear of God in the heart of Joseph he refused to give in. But unfortunately for Joseph one day when no one was at home, except himself and the wife of Potiphar, she caught Joseph by his garments to forcefully lie with him, but Joseph escaped. But his garment was left behind.

"And it came to pass about this time, that [Joseph] went into the house to do his business; and [there was] none of the men of the house there within. And she caught him by his garment, saying, Lie with me: and he left his garment in her hand, and fled, and got him out. And it came to pass, when she saw that he had left his garment in her hand, and was fled forth, That she called unto the men of her house, and spake unto them, saying, See, he hath brought in an Hebrew unto us to mock us; he came in unto me to lie with me, and I cried with a loud voice" (Genesis 39:11-14 KJV)

Once again Joseph's stripped garments were used against him, and he was sent to prison. In prison, he received prison garments. The reason why Joseph was convicted of rape was because of his garments. Joseph's status changed from a slave to a prisoner, and it all happened when his garments changed.

In the course of time, Joseph was needed at the palace to interpret Pharaoh, the king of Egypt's dream. His status and location were about to change. For that to happen his garments must first change.

"Then Pharaoh sent and called Joseph, and they brought him hastily out of the dungeon: and he shaved [himself], and changed his raiment, and came in unto Pharaoh" (Genesis 41:14 KJV)

As long as you wear prison garments, you can never go to the palace. You must wear palace garments to live and a stay in the palace. And those were the garments they put on Joseph.

Many people are born to live a Royal life, but spiritually they are wearing prison garments, and so they live from one prison to another prison and yet they belong to the palace. Even as you read this book, every prison garments the enemy put on you is removed in Jesus mighty name. Like Joseph, receive your royal garments.

Finally, Joseph received the ruler's garment or the kingly garment. You can be in the palace wearing royal garments, and you are not a ruler. But Joseph by divine favor became the ruler over all the land of Egypt, second only to Pharaoh. His royal garments were changed, and he wore rulers' garments.

"And Pharaoh said unto Joseph, See, I have set thee over all the land of Egypt. And Pharaoh took off his ring from his hand, and put it upon Joseph's hand, and arrayed him in vestures of fine linen, and put a gold chain about his neck" (Genesis 41:41-42 KJV)

So, the life of Joseph is consistent with the changes which occurred in his garments. When he had the coat of many colors, he enjoyed favor. When he lost it, he descended into a pit. From the pit, he received garments of slavery and became a slave. When the slavery garments were taken away, he received prison garments and stayed in prison. From the jail, they took away the prison garments, and he received royal garments. Because of the royal garments, he could access the palace. In the palace, he received the ruler's garment, and he obtained the throne. The alternation between Joseph's acquiring and losing garments is no coincidence. The Holy Spirit by the life of Joseph communicates to us the importance and significance of spiritual garments.

Beloved, before your level can change, your garments must change. You must give attention to the spiritual garments you are wearing because your garments determine the happenings around your life.

In the next chapter, we will examine specific types of evil or negative garments as revealed to us in the Scriptures.

CHAPTER 3

NEGATIVE OR EVIL GARMENTS

L et's prophetically examine some negative garments revealed in the scriptures and their manifestation and evil effects.

1. SACKCLOTH GARMENTS

The first garment we examine is the sackcloth garment. When that garment is put on you in the realms of the spirit, you will walk in depression and sadness. Everyone who suffers from depression is spiritually wearing sackcloth garment. If you can see with the eyes of a prophet, you can see that garment on anyone who walks in perpetual sadness and depression. This garment makes people mourn and sorrow in life. Let's examine these scriptures:

"O daughter of my people, gird [thee] with sackcloth, and wallow thyself in ashes: make thee mourning, [as for] an only son, most bitter lamentation: for the spoiler shall suddenly come upon us" (Jeremiah 6:26 KJV)

Jacob mourned when he wore the sackcloth garments:

"And Jacob rent his clothes, and put sackcloth upon his loins, and mourned for his son many days" (Genesis 37:34 KJV)

David and his men mourned for Abner, but before they mourned, they wore sackcloth:

"And David said to Joab, and to all the people that [were] with him, Rend your clothes, and gird you with sackcloth, and mourn before Abner. And king David [himself] followed the bier" (2 Samuel 3:31 KJV)

Anyone who is always moody, with no joy in their life are spiritually wearing sackcloth. The day those garments are removed, they will laugh and walk in joy. Till the sackcloth garments are lifted from you, no amount of antidepressant can help, because the source of the problem is spiritual. If you are suffering from any bout of depression in the name of Jesus, I remove the sackcloth garment over your life.

2. PRISON GARMENTS

When a person wears prison garments spiritually, his or her life remains in bondage. The day the spiritual prison garments are removed that person will be free to do what he or she was ordained to do. Jehoiachin, the king of Judah, was kept in prison by the king of Babylon. And in prison, he wore prison garments. Jehoiachin was a king and yet as long as he wore prison garments he was kept in bondage.

"And it came to pass in the seven and thirtieth year of the captivity of Jehoiachin king of Judah, in the twelfth month, on the seven and twentieth [day] of the month, [that] Evilmerodach king of Babylon in the year that he began to reign did lift up the <u>head of Jehoiachin king of Judah out of prison;</u> And he spake kindly to him, and set his throne above the throne of the kings that [were] with him in Babylon; <u>And changed his prison garments</u>: and he did eat bread continually before him all the days of his life" (2 Kings 25:27-29 KJV)

He was royalty and yet held in captivity. He had a great destiny and yet lacked expression because of the prison garments. The day the prison garments were taken away from Jehoiachin, he was spoken to kindly. Not only that, he did eat bread continually among the kings.

When you are wearing prison garments, people don't talk to you nicely. You are not treated with favor. You can't eat what you want to eat. You can't go where you want to go. You can't have what you want to have. You will start enjoying life when prison garments are taken from your life. It is possible your marriage is in prison. Your career or business can have prison garments cast upon it.

Right now, every prison garment over your life, marriage, family, children, ministry, career, business and destiny, by the power of the Holy Spirit I command them to catch fire and burn In Jesus mighty name. Nobody can put prison garments over your destiny. In Jesus mighty name. Amen

3. MOTH-EATEN GARMENTS

Moth-eaten garment is the garment eaten by the moth. When your spiritual garments are moth- eaten corruption comes into everything you do.

"Your riches are corrupted, and your garments are motheaten" (James 5:2 KJV)

The physical manifestation of this garment affects your riches and your possessions. Whatever you own begins to deteriorate with rapidity. You buy a phone today, and suddenly it gets broken. You pick up a car from the dealership, and before you get home, it fails to run. You buy a new dress, and it gets marked indelibly. Nothing you own lasts. And you seem not to comprehend it. It is not because you are careless. The source is spiritual. It is because of the moth-eaten garments.

The same moth-eaten garments can affect your health. Corruption creeps into your joints, bones and your organs. What is happening is that your moth-eaten garments are speaking against you because garments speak in the realm of the spirit. Until you handle it spiritually, it will continue.

4. NAKED GARMENTS

The next garment I want to bring to your attention is what I call Naked Garments. And you must understand the effect of this evil garment and handle it.

"Behold, I come as a thief. Blessed [is] he that watcheth, and keepeth his garments, lest he walk naked, and they see his shame" (Revelation 16:15 KJV)

When a person wears naked garments, spiritually shame and disgrace come to the person all the time. Most of the time if you have a dream and you are naked, it is a sign that you are wearing naked garments. It is a common dream many people have. I know this as a prophet because I have the privilege of counseling a lot of people and many people tend to have dreams where they are naked outside their house or even in a public place. Anytime you have such a dream; you don't have to say, you understand. Now you do. The devil wants to bring shame to you, your family, your ministry, your business or your career.

The enemy uses naked garments to attract and magnetize shame, disgrace, humiliation, and embarrassment to a person's life. There is another form of the naked garments which releases partial disgrace. The enemy uses this is to bring shame to specific areas of your life.

"Wherefore Hanun took David's servants, and shaved off the one half of their beards, and cut off their garments in the middle, [even] to their buttocks, and sent them away. When they told [it] unto David, he sent to meet them, because the men were greatly ashamed: and the king said, Tarry at Jericho until your beards be grown, and [then] return." (2 Samuel 10:4-5 KJV)

One day Hanun who was the Lord of the Ammonites caught the servants of King David. Instead of killing them, he decided to put them to shame and disgrace. He shaved their beard and cut off their garments at the buttocks exposing it and send them away. They were wearing garments, but parts of the garments were exposed. If a person has this type of spiritual garments what happens is that they can get every part of the life together but just one component brings disgrace. Your business might be doing well, but your marriage is nothing to write home about. Your children might be doing well, but your job is not well. The devil has cut portions of your life away so there are areas in your life you don't want to discuss.

5. STRIPPED-LIFE GARMENTS

The next garment we have to examine is very crucial for your existence on the earth. When your life garments are stripped away from you, death is imminent. This is connected to your preservation. God wanted Aaron to die, but as long as Aaron wore his holy garments which represented his life garments, he could not die. So, God told Moses to take Aaron up a mountain and strip him of his garments. The moment Moses stripped Aaron of his garments, he died.

"And strip Aaron of his garments, and put them upon Eleazar, his son: and Aaron shall be gathered [unto his people], and shall die there. And Moses did as the LORD commanded: and they went up into mount Hor in the sight of all the congregation. And Moses stripped Aaron of his garments, and put them upon Eleazar his son; and Aaron died there in the top of the mount: and Moses and Eleazar came down from the mount" (Numbers 20:26-28 KJV)

Aaron was very healthy. He was not sick, but just because he was stripped of his garments he died. In the realm of the spirit, most people who die prematurely have their garments stripped away from them. Most of the time when your life garments are stripped away, you are garmented with death garments. Whenever you dream and you see that your garments are being stripped from you, you must fight it and pray against it vehemently.

6. WIDOWHOOD GARMENTS

Now we have another spiritual garment called the widowhood garments. When the enemy manages to put it on you and nothing is done, you may lose your spouse. You can see these garments in scripture in when you examine them with a prophetic eye. The prophetic dimension of the scriptures opens to you new vistas.

Tamar wore a widowhood garment because she lost her husband. When she was ready for another marriage, she removed it.

"And she arose and went her way and laid by her vail from her, and put on the garments of her widowhood" (Genesis 38:19 KJV)

"And she put off from her, her widow's garments, and covered her with a vail, and wrapped herself, and sat in an open place, which is by the way to Timnath: for she saw that Shelah was grown, and she was

not given to him for a wife" (Genesis 38:14 KJV)

You can become an orphan as a child when orphan garments are put on you. When such garments are put on you, you lose loved ones. You must understand clearly that life is spiritual. Everything happens first in the spirit before manifestation.

7. VILE GARMENTS (POVERTY GARMENTS)

When a person has vile garments on spiritually, the person stays in poverty perpetually. Till that garment is removed spiritually, nothing changes.

"For if there come unto your assembly a man with a gold ring, in goodly apparel, and there come in also a poor man in vile raiment" (James 2:2 KJV)

In the realm of the spirit when you have vile garments on, you can be given a million dollars, yet you will lose all. You can work double jobs and yet still has nothing to show for it. What brings prosperity to everybody, you will try, and get nothing. But thank God that in the name of Jesus, you can change your garments.

8. BEGGAR GARMENTS

Very connected to poverty garments is what is called the beggar's garments. Once you have this garment on spiritually, you keep begging all your life.

There was a blind beggar called Bartimaeus. He has been begging all his life because he was blind. One day he heard Jesus, the miracle worker, who can change his life was passing his way. When Jesus called him to come to him so that he can change his level and circumstances, the first thing Bartimaeus did was to cast away the beggarly garments he had on. And that was the last day he ever begged.

"And many charged him that he should hold his peace: but he cried the more a great deal, [Thou] Son of David, have mercy on me. And Jesus stood still, and commanded him to be called. And they call the blind man, saying unto him, Be of good comfort, rise; he calleth thee. And he, casting away his garment, rose, and came to Jesus" (Mark 10:48-50 KJV)

Beloved, for your circumstances to change physically or for you to have a change of level, you must have a change of garments as it was in the case of Bartimaeus. Till your garments change, there is no change of level. It will not matter how much you push in the physical.

9. COBWEBS GARMENTS

Many people complain of feeling engulfed in cobwebs when walking outside in public places where you are sure no spider can weave its web. You might have even experienced that before or you are still experiencing it. It is a demonic spiritual garment called "Cobweb

Garments" which the enemy puts on a lot of people.

"Their cobwebs are useless for clothing; they cannot cover themselves with what they make. Their deeds are evil deeds, and acts of violence are in their hands" (Isaiah 59:6 KJV)

"Their webs shall not become garments, neither shall they cover themselves with their works: their works [are] works of iniquity, and the act of violence [is] in their hands" (Isaiah 59:6 KJV)

The above scripture declares that their webs will not become garments. The reason the enemy throws around you cobwebs is to weave or spin for you a demonic garment. If you don't handle the cobwebs, the enemy will weave for you garments of violence, disease, disappointment, failure, disaster and whatever he wants to throw at you.

The enemy casts this garment on people mostly when they are close to a miracle or a great opportunity. At times just before an interview, a person will feel cobweb garments come upon them.

10. FILTHY GARMENTS

Filthy garments are garments soiled by sin. When you commit any wrongdoing, your garments become filthy spiritually. When a person has filthy garments, he/she is accused in the realm of the spirit based on that garment.

"Now Joshua was clothed with filthy garments, and stood before the angel. And he answered and spake unto those that stood before him, saying, Take away the filthy garments from him. And unto him he said, Behold, I have caused thine iniquity to pass from thee, and I will clothe thee with change of raiment" **(Zechariah 3:3-4 KJV)**

So that the devil who is the accuser of the brethren, does not accuse us based on filthy garments, Jesus gave us his blood. Any time we sin, and we plead the blood it will cleanse us and make us as white as snow.

"Come now, and let us reason together, saith the LORD: though your sins be as scarlet, they shall be as white as snow; though they be red like crimson, they shall be as wool" (Isaiah 1:18 KJV)

It is the blood of Jesus that cleanses us and make us white as snow and clean as wool.

".....and the blood of Jesus Christ his Son cleanseth us from all sin" (1 John 1:7 KJV)

Use the blood of Jesus to take care of every filthy garment.

In the next chapter, we will examine certain good spiritual garments you can change into for a dramatic turnaround.

CHAPTER 4

POSITIVE OR GOOD GARMENTS

In this chapter, we will understand and discover by divine revelation some of the positive garments God has made provision for us in scriptures and what they do.

1. BEAUTIFUL GARMENTS

The first garments we will look at is Beautiful garments.

"Awake, awake; put on thy strength, O Zion; put on thy beautiful garments, O Jerusalem, the holy city: for henceforth there shall no more come into thee the uncircumcised and the unclean" (Isaiah 52:1 KJV)

The scriptures instruct us to put on our beautiful garments. In the realm of the spirit, you have a garment called Beautiful Garments. And you must put them on. When you put on your beautiful garments two things happen. First, your strength is intact. Your physical and your spiritual strength increases. You are also strengthened emotionally too. When you fail to put them on, your health comes under attack. You grow weaker by the day. But that is not the will of God for your life. God wants your strength to increase by the day.

"….and as thy days, [so shall] thy strength [be]" (Deuteronomy 33:25 KJV)

Secondly, when you put on beautiful garments nothing unclean or ugly comes around your life. People are careful to treat you with contempt when you wear beautiful garments. Your dignity grows and your splendor in life glows more. Learn to array yourself with beautiful garments in the spirit. You can be wearing the latest designer fashion in town, but if spiritually you lack beautiful garments ugly things will happen to you your designer garments notwithstanding.

2. PERFUMED GARMENTS

In the physical realm, many people wear perfumes before they step out. Everyone wants to smell good. When you are in a room, and someone smells good, everybody is attracted to the person, and when anyone smells bad too, everyone moves away from that person or individual. Nobody wants to stay around a bad stench.

In the realm of the spirit too, there is a garment called Perfumed garments. When you wear such garments, you attract good things to yourself. You are treated favorably.

"All thy garments [smell] of myrrh, and aloes, [and] cassia, out of the ivory palaces, whereby they have made thee glad" (Psalms 45:8 KJV)

"Myrrh, aloes, and cassia perfume your robes. In ivory palaces, the music of strings entertains you" (Psalms 45:8 NLT)

When you put on perfumed garments, glad tidings come to you all the time. Secondly, you walk in favor. You attract and magnetize things. People give you gifts all the time. When you walk with perfumed garments, your life is like living in an ivory palace. Make sure you always put on your perfumed garments. It will make your life glorious.

The secret of walking in great blessing is by putting on perfumed garments. When Isaac was ready to bless Jacob, the first thing he did was to smell the garments of Jacob to see which type of odor he emitted. When he verified that Jacob emitted a good smell, he blessed him. I believe if he had gotten a bad smell, he would have restrained from blessing him.

"So he went to him and kissed him. When Isaac caught the smell of his clothes, he blessed him and said, "Ah, the smell of my son is like the smell of a field that the LORD has blessed" (Genesis 27:27 KJV)

The blessing of the Lord rests upon you when your spiritual garments are perfumed. You attract blessings everywhere you go. When your garments are not perfumed, even your spouse will move away from you. You will lack favor in the sight of your superiors and neighbors.

3. PRAISE GARMENTS

Praise garments are very powerful garments in the realm of the spirit. And you must consciously put them on constantly.

"To appoint unto them that mourn in Zion, to give unto them beauty for ashes, the oil of joy for mourning, the garment of praise for the spirit of heaviness; that they might be called trees of righteousness, the planting of the LORD, that he might be glorified" (Isaiah 61:3 KJV)

The first thing that happens when you wear praise garments is that you receive beauty instead of ashes. Instead of men casting ashes on you, you will receive a bouquet of roses. Your life becomes wonderful. The next thing is that you receive the oil of joy. When the oil of Joy rests on you, depression, sadness and mourning leave your life. The spirit of heaviness cannot manifest in the life of the person who wears the praise garments.

One sign that you are wearing praise garments is that complaining and murmuring cease from your life. Instead of complaining, you sing songs of praise and adoration. Such a person becomes a tree of righteousness and the planting of the Lord. Endeavor to put on your praise garments always as it is the secret to establishment and advancement. It is also the secret to winning all the battles of life.

King David was a man who always had his praise garments on. He praised God seven times a day instead of complaining.

"Seven times a day do I praise thee because of thy righteous judgments" (Psalms 119:164 KJV)

No wonder he was the only King who never lost a battle.

4. GARMENTS OF SALVATION/ROBE OF RIGHTEOUSNESS

Everyone who is born again, or a Christian has garments of salvation on. It is a special garment given to only believers. The unbeliever does not have it. And it makes you unique in the spiritual realm.

"I will greatly rejoice in the LORD, my soul shall be joyful in my God; for he hath clothed me with the garments of salvation, he hath covered me with the robe of righteousness, as a bridegroom decketh [himself] with ornaments, and as a bride adorneth [herself] with her jewels" (Isaiah 61:10 KJV)

Garments of salvation always come along with the robe of righteousness. Righteousness is a gift for every believer. **"For if by one man's offense death reigned by one; much**

more they which receive abundance of grace and of the gift of righteousness shall reign in life by one, Jesus Christ." (Romans 5:17 KJV)

It is the garments of salvation and the robe of righteousness that makes you worthy to be the bride of Christ. This garment comes with ornaments and jewels of all types.

Every Christian should walk in the consciousness that he is arrayed with the garments of salvation and the robe of righteousness. This will set you apart from the filth of sin and decadence in the world.

5. SHINING GARMENTS

"And it came to pass, as they were much perplexed thereabout, behold, two men stood by them in shining garments" (Luke 24:4 KJV)

Shining garments make you stand out in the affairs of life. The Bible declares that you are the light of the world.

"Ye are the light of the world. A city that is set on an hill cannot be hid" (Matthew 5:14 KJV)

When you are wearing shining garments, you cannot be hid. You don't become a nonentity or a mediocre. Always deck and adorn yourself with shining garments.

6. ANOINTED GARMENTS

Anointed garments are special garments which have been soaked in the anointing of the Holy Spirit. These garments have been imparted with God's ability. Anointed garments are impregnated with miracle-working power. Such garments have come into contact with anointed men of God. Clothes worn by men of God to minister fall into this category of garments.

Let me give you examples of such garments in the Scriptures.

The garments of Jesus were anointed garments because Jesus was the Christ. He was the Anointing Himself.

"And, behold, a woman, which was diseased with an issue of blood twelve years, came behind [him], and touched the hem of his garment: For she said within herself, If I may but touch his garment, I shall be whole. But Jesus turned him about, and when he saw her, he said, Daughter, be of good comfort; thy faith hath made thee whole. And the woman was made whole from that hour" (Matthew 9:20-22 KJV)

The woman with the issue of blood touched the hem of Jesus' garments and received her healing. The garments of Jesus had received an impartation of the anointing on the life of Jesus.

Jesus wasn't the only one to produce anointed garments. Paul, the apostle, also produced anointed garments.

"So that from his body were brought unto the sick handkerchiefs or aprons, and the diseases departed from them, and the evil spirits went out of them" (Acts 19:12 KJV)

The handkerchiefs and garments which Paul laid hands on became pregnant with the anointing. The garments did cast out devils and healed diseases in the absence of Paul because it carried the same amount of energy the apostle carried.

Beloved, learn to value the items which have received impartations from anointed men of God. They can heal and cause miraculous changes in your life.

CHAPTER 5

PRAYER POINTS

I believe you might have asked how to get rid of evil garments and put on good garments. Use these prayer points as a guide to pray and adorn yourself with the proper spiritual garments.

Heavenly Father, I stand in the blood of Jesus and on the authority of your word, and I declare:

1. By the blood of the lamb, I am washed and cleansed from every sin. Every filthy garment is removed from me now. I put on my garments of salvation and my robes of righteousness. In Jesus mighty name.

2. Every naked and disgraceful garment the evil one has put on me to cause me to walk in shame and disgrace I command it to be removed right now and catch fire. In

Jesus mighty name.

3. My Father, my Maker, every death garment and widowhood garments the enemy has cast upon me, or anyone close to me I remove it violently, and I cause it to catch fire right now. In Jesus mighty name.

4. I declare in the mighty name of Jesus that no evil spirit or evil man can strip me of my life garments. I am preserved in the name of the Lord.

5. Every sackcloth garments cast upon my life which brings sorrows, sadness, and depression in my life, I remove them now by the power of the Holy Ghost, and I command them to burn by the fire of the Holy Ghost. In Jesus mighty name.

6. Every garment of poverty over my destiny be removed right now and catch fire.

7. Every beggarly garment that causes me to beg and stay in debt, right now in the mighty name of Jesus, be removed and catch fire.

8. Every moth-eaten garment which brings corruption into my life, my properties, and my body, I cast it off, and I command it to catch fire right now. In Jesus mighty name.

9. Every prison garment that has held me bound and stagnated, I remove it, destroy it and cast it into the fire of the Holy Ghost.

10. Every demonic cobweb against my life, my marriage, family, ministry or business I command them to catch fire right now.

11. Now in the name of Jesus, I put on my beautiful garments of strength. I establish that nothing unclean or uncircumcised come near my dwelling.

12. I declare that from today all my garments are perfumed and fragrant with myrrh. I attract favor, increase, money and everything good treasure in Jesus mighty name.

13. I declare in the name of Jesus Christ that all my garments are specially anointed with the Holy Ghost and with power. I go about doing good and healing all that are oppressed of the devil.

14. I declare that from today I manifest with my shining garments. I arise and can never be hid in the course of life. In Jesus mighty name.

15. I put on my garments of praise all day long. I refuse to worry or complain. I have the oil of joy resting upon me. In Jesus mighty name.

16. I declare I am garmented in heaven's royalty with all the beauties of Christ in Jesus mighty name.

Finally, dear reader, I pray for you:

From my office as a prophet, I lift and remove every garment of death, failure, depression over your life. I lose you from garments of poverty and corruption right now.

And right now, I release garments of greatness, prosperity, gladness acceptance, advancement, opportunities, progress and blessings over your life. Receive them now In Jesus mighty name. Amen.

Made in the
USA
Lexington, KY

54487758R00035